★ ★ ★

THE U.S. AIR FORCE

THE U.S. AIR FORCE

BY ROSE BLUE AND
CORINNE J. NADEN

Defending Our Country
The Millbrook Press
Brookfield, Connecticut

From Rose:

*To my good friend Al Schwartz, handsome,
dashing airman, a true officer and a gentleman*

From Corinne:

*To my dear friend, ex-pilot Harold C. Vaughan,
with love*

Cover photographs courtesy of U.S. Air Force
Photographs courtesy of U.S. Air Force except: U.S. Army:
p. 9; FPG International: pp. 33, 34; Bettmann: p. 41, 44, 49,
50–51, 53 (top); New York Public Library Picture Collection:
p. 46; Wide World: p. 53 (bottom).

Library of Congress Cataloging-in-Publication Data
Blue, Rose.
The U.S. Air Force / by Rose Blue and Corinne J. Naden.
p.   cm. — (Defending our country)
Includes bibliographical references (p.   ) and index.
Summary: Surveys the history, role, planes, weapons, command
structure, and work of the United States Air Force.
ISBN 1-56294-217-4 (lib. bdg.)
ISBN 1-56294-754-0 (pbk.)
1. United States.   Air Force—Juvenile literature.   [1. United
States. Air Force.]   I. Naden, Corinne J.   II. Title.   III. Title:
US Air Force.   IV. Series.
UG633.B63   1993
358.4'00973—dc20   92-13431   CIP   AC

Published by The Millbrook Press
2 Old New Milford Road
Brookfield, Connecticut 06804

CONTENTS

I
Introduction: From the *Flyer* to the Falcon 7

II
What the Air Force Does and How It Does It 11

III
Modern Planes and Weapons 22

IV
Men and Women of the Air Force 32

V
The Air Force Then and Now 40

Important Events in Air Force History 57
Air Force Talk 59
Books for Further Reading 61
Index 62

INTRODUCTION: FROM THE *FLYER* TO THE *FALCON*

It was a windy December day on Kill Devil Hill. There was nothing unusual about that. It was always a windy day on Kill Devil Hill. In fact, that's why the U.S. Weather Bureau had recommended this area near Kitty Hawk, North Carolina, as the perfect site to test the inventors' latest idea—an airplane.

The date was December 17,1903. The inventors were Wilbur and Orville Wright. Back home in Dayton, Ohio, they were successful bicycle makers. They were also inventors, and for a number of years they had been studying flight. Lots of people had long tried to do what birds do so easily. They had all failed. Using the records of earlier inventors, the Wright brothers built and tested a man-carrying kite. From 1900 to 1902, test after test failed.

Perhaps the earlier inventors were on the wrong track. The Wrights came up with a new idea. They built the world's first wind tunnel from an old laundry starch box. They put wings of different shapes into the box and blew air over them. In this way they were able to find out which wing shapes gave the most lift, meaning which best stayed up in the air.

All during the winter of 1902–1903, Orville and Wilbur tested wing shapes. They built a second, more efficient wind tunnel run by a gasoline engine. After about two hundred tests, the bicycle makers from Dayton decided to build a new glider. They tested it about one thousand times.

Now the Wrights built their first self-propelled, heavier-than-air machine. Called the *Flyer,* it was a biplane—a plane with two sets of wings, one above the other. It also had two propellers powered by a gasoline engine.

Wilbur and Orville were ready for their big test in the fall of 1903. On December 14, Wilbur, the older brother, took off from Kill Devil Hill. He and the *Flyer* crashed after three and a half seconds. Fortunately, Wilbur wasn't badly hurt.

The *Flyer* needed some repairs, but it was ready for the next test on the morning of December 17, 1903. This time it was the younger Wright's turn. Orville climbed aboard the *Flyer* and took off into the wind of Kill Devil Hill.

The *Flyer* stayed in the air for twelve seconds and flew 120 feet (36 meters)! This was the first successful flight by an airplane.

In 1909 the Wright brothers supplied the U.S. Army with its first airplane. It carried two men and flew at about 40 miles (64 kilometers) per hour. Its range was 125 miles (200 kilometers). What changes there have been in American military planes since that day in 1909! Today, many Air Force planes, such as the F-16B Falcon, still carry two people. But that's the only similarity. During a combat mission, the Falcon's range is 575 miles (925 kilometers). On a regular flight, though, it can fly for more than 2,400 miles (3,860 kilometers). And it can fly at more than twice the speed of sound—or almost forty times

Orville Wright and U.S. Army lieutenant Thomas
E. Selfridge about to take off on a test flight on
September 17, 1908. Selfridge died when the plane
crashed, but Wright survived.

faster than the Wright brothers' airplane. This outstanding plane is flown by the Thunderbirds, the Air Force demonstration team that thrills spectators at air shows.

The story of the growth of aviation from the Wright brothers' *Flyer* to the Thunderbirds' Falcon is also the story of the military service that is the United States Air Force.

Planes such as this F-16 help make the modern U.S. Air Force the most powerful the world has ever known.

★ ★ ★

WHAT THE AIR FORCE DOES AND HOW IT DOES IT

The job of the United States Air Force (USAF) is to protect the United States from any threat by air and to defeat aggressors. Along with the Army, Navy, and Marine Corps, the Air Force is pledged to preserve the peace and security of the United States and to defend it if necessary.

To carry out its mission, the Air Force must have aircraft and missiles that can prevent or fight a war, land-based forces that can intercept an enemy and give support to combat troops on the ground, aerospace forces to defend against a possible air and missile attack, and equipment to lift troops and supplies by air for use by all the U.S. military branches. In addition, the Air Force conducts major research and development projects and assists the National Aeronautics and Space Administration (NASA) in conducting the U.S. space program.

The Air Force is the youngest of all U.S. military services. Its birth date is September 18, 1947. On that day, the National Security Act became law. Signed by President Harry Truman, it set up the

The Air Force mission requires a wide range of skills and equipment. Here, a KC-135 stratotanker prepares to refuel an F-15 in flight.

National Military Establishment, which was renamed the Department of Defense (DOD) in 1949.

The DOD was divided into three equal branches. The former War Department became the Department of the Army. The Navy Department became the Department of the Navy, which included the Marine Corps. And a brand-new branch was created—the Department of the Air Force.

The seal of
the U.S. Air Force.

The head of the Department of Defense is a civilian—the secretary of defense. Each of the three branches is also headed by a civilian secretary. The first secretary of the Air Force was Stuart Symington, who had been an assistant secretary of war and who later became a U.S. senator from Missouri. The highest-ranking military officer in the Air Force is the chief of staff. The first chief of staff was General Carl "Tooey" Spaatz, a World War II veteran.

All American military forces are commanded by the Joint Chiefs of Staff (JCS). This group meets weekly in Washington, D.C. It includes a chairman and vice chairman, the chief of naval operations, the commandant of the Marine Corps, and the chiefs of staff of the Army and Air Force. These six people advise the president in decisions about the military. The president is commander in chief of all the military forces.

The Air Force doesn't decide how much money it will spend, or how many people it will keep on active duty, or even how many generals it can have. Congress sets the budget for all the U.S. military and regulates the number of personnel.

The Air Force may be the youngest military branch, but it is awesome indeed. It includes more than 500,000 servicemen and women on active duty. In addition, there are more than 250,000 men and women in the Air Force Reserve and the Air National Guard. The Air Force Reserve has its headquarters at Robins Air Force Base (AFB) in Georgia and has units all around the country. Its members are not on active duty, but they stay in training and can be called into service in an emergency. Some reserve units of the Air Force, as well as the Army and Navy, were activated during the war in the Persian Gulf in 1991.

Units of the Air National Guard operate in all fifty states. They can also be called into service in a national emergency. Guard units may be asked to stop riots, fight forest fires, or help the injured after floods, hurricanes, or other disasters in the United States.

The USAF also employs thousands of civilians. It operates about 140 air bases and installations all around the United States and the world.

How does the Air Force do it?

It does it by organizing. To keep this huge military branch operating smoothly, the Air Force is divided into Headquarters, Major Commands, Field Operating Agencies, and Direct Reporting Units.

Air Force Headquarters is located in the Pentagon building in Washington, D.C., as are the headquarters for all the military services. Headquarters sets policy, reviews programs, plans and budgets, and distributes resources to all Air Force units. It is the center of all Air Force activities.

★ Air Force Commands

For years, one of the main jobs of the Air Force and the other services was to counter the threat of nuclear war with the Soviet Union. But in 1991, the Soviet Union collapsed. As the threat of nuclear war grew less, military budgets were cut. In 1991 the Air Force began a streamlining project. Over the next few years, it planned to decrease in size, as did all military branches. The Air Force made plans to close down twenty-five of its bases and to reduce the number of active-duty personnel by 81,000. In addition, in 1992 it was announced that there would be major cuts in reserve forces.

Changes in technology have also changed the way the Air Force will operate in the future. ''Global reach—global power'' might be thought of as its new slogan. This policy focuses on the speed, range, and flexibility of air power. It dedicates the Air Force to operate anywhere in the world, as it did during the war in the Persian Gulf in 1991.

In this new ''leaner, meaner'' Air Force, these are the major commands:

Air Combat Command, Langley AFB, Virginia, is in charge of fighters, bombers, and intercontinental ballistic missiles (ICBMs), which are called ''shooters.'' Before the Air Force's reorganization, most fighters were under the control of the Tactical Air Command. And the Strategic Air Command controlled the bombers and long-range missiles. These two commands were phased out when the Air Force reorganized.

The Air Force Air Combat Command oversees missiles like this Minuteman, shown in a test launch, as well as fighters and bombers.

AIR FORCE ONE

The most famous plane in the United States must be the huge Boeing 747 known as Air Force One. This is the beautiful white jet you see whenever the president of the United States flies off to some part of the country or the world. It looks presidential, indeed, with the bold letters UNITED STATES OF AMERICA on its side and the American flag painted on its tail.

Actually, Air Force One is two planes, tail numbers 28000 and 29000. They are part of the 89th Military Airlift Wing at Andrews Air Force Base in Maryland. Whichever plane the president flies in uses the radio call sign of Air Force One.

The president's plane can carry seventy-three passengers and an amazing array of electronic and communications equipment. It can cruise at up to 630 miles (1,000 kilometers) per hour and can refuel in air. In addition to an office and conference/dining room, Air Force One has a presidential suite with a dressing room and shower. It has six passenger bathrooms, two kitchens (called galleys), in which one hundred meals at a time can be prepared, space for news personnel and the Secret Service, and a rest area for the crew.

Air Mobility Command, Scott AFB, Illinois, controls most of the tanker force and airlift planes.

Air Force Intelligence Command, Kelly AFB, San Antonio, Texas, combines intelligence operations once scattered among other commands.

Air Force Matériel Command, Wright-Patterson AFB, Ohio, makes sure that Air Force units everywhere have the supplies they need. It buys, stores, supplies, and transports anything the Air Force needs anywhere, including about 890,000 airplane parts.

Air Force Space Command, Peterson AFB, Colorado, is in charge of Air Force space programs. It was created in 1982. The Space Command works with NASA on U.S. space projects, including the operation of the space shuttle. And it is responsible for early warning of an enemy air attack. It also keeps track of weather and communications satellites as well as ''space junk,'' pieces of rockets or satellites left in orbit.

Air Force Special Operations Command, Hurlburt Field, Florida, has as its motto ''Air Commandos—Quiet Professionals.'' Its mission is to organize, train, equip, and educate special operations units of the Air Force. This would include such unconventional warfare as dealing with terrorism.

Air Training Command, Randolph AFB, Texas, recruits and trains airmen and officers for the Air Force. Since it was created in 1943 during World War II, it has trained more than ten million people! Anyone who joins the Air Force will at some time be trained by this command. It provides, among other things, basic military and officer training (at Lackland AFB, Texas), reserve officer training (headquarters Maxwell AFB, Alabama), and technical training in nearly 350 different fields at six centers in Colorado, Illinois, Mississippi, and Texas. This command also runs a fifty-two-week pilot training pro-

An instructor in an Air Force pilot training program.

gram at five bases in Arizona, Mississippi, Oklahoma, and Texas; navigator school at Mather AFB, California; and space training for specialists at Lowry AFB, Colorado.

Air University, Maxwell AFB, Alabama, sees to the higher education of Air Force officers at various locations around the country. It may be thought of as the Air Force Academy's graduate school.

Pacific Air Force, Hickam AFB, Hawaii, provides the U.S. Pacific Command with everything it needs for air combat.

United States Air Forces in Europe, Ramstein AFB, Germany, provides the U.S. European Command with what it needs for air combat.

The thirty-four Field Operating Agencies include such units as the Air Weather Service, the Civilian Personnel Management Center, and the Air Force Reserve. The three Direct Reporting Units are the Air Force District of Washington, the Air Force Operational Test and Evaluation Center, and the United States Air Force Academy.

The basic fighting unit of the Air Force has always been and continues to be the wing. A wing is stationed at one base and has one commander. Some wings operate only one kind of aircraft, such as fighters or bombers. Others are composite wings. They might have, for example, fighters, tankers, and special-mission craft. They are designed to get to trouble spots in a hurry anywhere in the world, another example of "global reach—global power."

★ ★ ★

MODERN PLANES AND WEAPONS

During the Civil War in the 1860s, the Union Army's "air force" consisted of a few balloons. Today the Air Force keeps nearly seven thousand aircraft ready to fly, as well as hundreds of long-range missiles.

Planes are designated with letters and numbers, such as F-111 or B-52. The letters show the type of plane, such as F for fighter or B for bomber. The numbers are the model number. Actually, you can tell a lot about one plane by reading all the information on its tail. "AF," of course, stands for Air Force. Suppose you see the large letters "MO." That means the plane is stationed at Mountain Home AFB in Idaho. "NY" means Hancock Field, New York. If you saw an F-111 with the numbers "67-0021," you would know you were looking at the twenty-first fighter bought in 1967.

Air Force planes are organized into squadrons, each with a certain number of planes and each with its own facilities. A B-52 squadron, for instance, may have from thirteen to nineteen bombers. An F-111 squadron may have from twelve to twenty-four fighters. Besides bomber and fighter squadrons, there are weather, rescue, electronic warfare, and other types of squadrons. There are nearly four hundred squadrons in all, including the reserve units.

Aircraft

Modern planes of the Air Force can be divided into bombers, fighters, attack and observation planes, reconnaissance and special-duty craft, transports and tankers, trainers, and helicopters.

Bombers are the "big guns" of the Air Force. They are generally the most visible and the largest of the USAF planes. Their function is to drop explosives on enemy targets. First, radar helps direct the plane to the target; then the navigator releases the bombs.

The Air Force has almost 400 bombers, of which 262 are B-52s. Most of these are at least thirty years old. The B-52 is called the Stratofortress. It is a long-range, heavy bomber. This sleek eight-engine jet with its swept-back wings carries a crew of six. It can refuel in the air. But even without refueling, the B-52G can travel more than 7,500 miles (12,100 kilometers), and the B-52H about 8,800 miles (14,200 kilometers).

The B-1, a four-engine bomber, is designed to fly at low levels at subsonic speeds (less than the speed of sound). With a crew of four, it has a range of more than 6,000 miles (9,700 kilometers).

The most advanced of the USAF bombers is the B-2. It is known as the "stealth" bomber because it is supposed to be extremely difficult to pick up on enemy radar. It carries a crew of two and was first unveiled in 1988. Its design makes it look like a craft from the next century. Because of budget cuts, the Air Force will get only twenty of these planes instead of the seventy-five originally planned.

**Air Force bombers:
The B-52 (above),
and the newer B-1.**

**The F-117 uses "stealth" technology
to elude enemy radar.**

A *fighter* plane shoots down enemy aircraft and attacks ground targets. The Air Force has about 2,500 fighters, more than any other type of plane. The needle-nose F-15 Eagle, for example, is a single-seater that flies at more than twice the speed of sound. The F-16 Fighting Falcon has one- and two-seat models. The pilot sits in a bubble canopy for greater vision. The F-117 Stealth fighter, like the B-2 bomber, is able to elude enemy radar. It carries laser- and video-guided bombs known as "smart" bombs. The F-111 is another important Air Force fighter plane. It has a range of almost 3,000 miles (4,800 kilometers) and can be used as a medium-range bomber.

THE FASTEST PLANE
IN THE WORLD

The Lockheed SR-71, known as the "Blackbird" because it is painted black, is the fastest plane in the world. It can fly at more than three times the speed of sound. The first SR-71 was built in 1966, and five more followed.

The SR-71, the world's fastest plane.

They were based at Beale Air Force Base in California. In 1989, the Air Force took them out of service—or, in Air Force language, they were "mothballed." Before then, however, the SR-71 set some impressive performance records. In 1976, Air Force Captain Elden Joersz flew an SR-71 at 2,193.16 miles (3,528.79 kilometers) an hour. The Blackbird is also the highest-flying plane in the world. When on a mission, it would fly at an altitude of more than 15 miles (24 kilometers).

The Blackbird carries a crew of two, but it has no armaments. This is because it is a reconnaissance plane, not a fighter or bomber. Reconnaissance planes photograph and observe enemy forces. The SR-71 is so fast it could cover an area the size of Colorado or Wyoming in just an hour.

Attack and observation planes aid ground troops with air support and keep an eye on enemy troops and movements. The A-10 Thunderbolt II is a single-seat twin jet that can land and take off on short runways, allowing it to operate near enemy lines.

Reconnaissance and special-duty aircraft observe and photograph enemy bases and positions and survey weather conditions, among other duties. The E-3 Sentry (called AWACS—for *a*irborne *w*arning *a*nd *c*ontrol *s*ystem) is a rather strange-looking Boeing 707 commercial plane with a huge rotating radar dome on top. It carries a crew of four but has room for up to nineteen specialists on a mission. Its electronic gear can gather information in a 200-mile (322-kilometer) range. The Air Force has thirty-eight AWACS in operation.

A ground crew prepares an AWACS plane for takeoff. The plane's sensitive radar and electronic gear can monitor a wide area.

Transports and tankers keep the Air Force moving with personnel and supplies. The Air Force has more than 1,500 of them. Many are used to refuel bombers and fighters in midair. The KC-135 Strato-tanker refuels long-range bombers. It carries a crew of four with 120,000 pounds (54,500 kilograms) of transfer fuel. The fuel is pumped from the tanker into the flying aircraft through a boom, which is controlled by an operator at the rear of the plane.

Among the transport planes is the C-9A Nightingale, a twin-engine jet with a crew of eight, including two nurses and three aeromedical technicians. Designed to carry patients and medical personnel, it has room for forty stretchers, called litters in the military. The C5A/B Galaxy is the largest plane in the Western world. The Air Force has more than 125 of these giant planes. Each one can carry 345 soldiers.

The Air Force has about 1,500 *trainers* that are used to instruct future pilots and navigators. One of them, the twin-engine T-37 Tweet. in different models, has been in Air Force use since 1957. The Air Force also operates about 200 *helicopters,* such as the general purpose, twin-engine UH-1N Iroquois. Helicopters are especially valuable for transporting troops into combat areas or behind enemy lines, rescuing downed pilots at sea, and other special missions.

★ Missiles

Aircraft, of course, are what the Air Force is all about. But next to its planes, the most important Air Force weapon is the missile. A guided missile is an unmanned vehicle that travels through the atmosphere.

A helicopter is unloaded
from a C-5 transport.

Unlike a cannon shell, for instance, the guided missile contains some mechanism for controlling its flight. Missiles can be fitted with a conventional or nuclear warhead.

The *air interceptor missile (AIM)*, or air-to-air missile, is fired by an aircraft against an enemy plane. The Sidewinder is a supersonic AIM carried by Air Force fighter planes.

The *air-to-surface missile (ASM)* is fired by an aircraft at a ground target. Among these is the delta-wing Maverick missile, which has been used by the Air Force since 1983. A *surface-to-surface* missile is fired from the ground at an enemy ground target. The largest of these missiles is the *ICBM* (*int*ercontinental *b*allistic *m*issile). The first test flight of the Peacekeeper, in 1983, sent this ICBM successfully from Vandenberg AFB in California to a range nearly 4,200 miles (6,800 kilometers) away in the Pacific Ocean.

Beyond the range of its planes and missiles, the USAF is also involved with its newest frontier—space. Included in its space fleet are Atlas and Titan launch vehicles and the Space Transportation System (STS), which most people call simply the space shuttle.

A test firing of a Peacekeeper missile, which has a range of thousands of miles.

IV

★ ★ ★

MEN AND WOMEN
OF THE AIR FORCE

Today, more than 500,000 men and women wear the ultramarine blue of the United States Air Force. That number should decrease through the 1990s.

Air Force men and women are part of what is sometimes called the ''glamorous'' military service. Just say the words ''Air Force'' and you think of sleek jet planes roaring off into the ''wild blue yonder,'' or silvery airships streaking into space, or dashing young pilots with silver wings pinned to their uniforms. Actually, only a small percentage of Air Force personnel ride those jets into the sky. There are fewer than 20,000 pilots out of a total of some 90,000 Air Force officers.

★ Officers

No matter what their job, the elite of the U.S. Air Force officer corps are the graduates of the Air Force Academy.

Air Force men and women fill many jobs.
These are air traffic controllers.

Cadets toss their hats in the air at Air Force
Academy graduation ceremonies.

Not surprisingly, the youngest of the U.S. military services has the youngest military academy. The oldest is the Army's U.S. Military Academy (1802) at West Point, New York, followed by the Naval Academy (1845) at Annapolis, Maryland, and the Coast Guard Academy (1876) at New London, Connecticut. After the Air Force became an independent branch of service in 1947, plans began for opening an academy. But it was not until April 1, 1954, that President Dwight D. Eisenhower signed the Academy Act.

The first class of 306 cadets met on July 11, 1955, at Lowry Air Force Base near Denver, Colorado. In August 1958 the academy moved to its permanent home—8 miles (13 kilometers) north of Colorado Springs on 18,000 acres (7,300 hectares) in the beautiful foothills of the Rocky Mountains. The first class, by then reduced to 207 young men, graduated in June 1959.

By 1964 the academy had expanded to 4,417 students. In 1992, however, Congress ordered the academy to reduce enrollment to 4,000 by 1995. The students are known as the Cadet Wing. Minorities make up about fifteen percent of the Cadet Wing, and women about twelve percent. Women were admitted to the academy in 1976, and the class of 1980 boasted its first women graduates. Women also make up about twelve percent of all Air Force officers and about ten percent of all Air Force personnel.

Each year some 12,000 to 16,000 young men and women apply for admission to the Air Force Academy. Only 1,200 to 1,600 are accepted. Cadets must be American citizens, unmarried, and in good physical shape. And they must have good high school grades, usually in the top twenty percent. They also must pass qualifying exams. The first step in applying for admission is to write to your senator or representative to sponsor your nomination.

The mission of the Air Force Academy is to "provide instruction and experience to all cadets so they graduate with the knowledge, character, and motivation essential to leadership as career officers in the United States Air Force.'' To complete that mission, cadets spend four years at the academy and earn a Bachelor of Science degree. They can select from twenty-five different career majors. About half of them choose science or engineering. Most of the nearly six hundred teachers at the academy are Air Force officers.

Education at the Air Force Academy is free. So is housing, food, and medical care. Cadets are also given money for uniforms, textbooks, and other expenses. Life at the academy is disciplined and strict. The cadets live by an honor code that says ''We will not lie, steal, or cheat, nor tolerate among us anyone who does.'' The weekday begins at 6:30 A.M. and is filled with inspections, meals, eight hours of classes, and a three-hour study period until taps is sounded at 11:00 P.M.

Every member of the Cadet Wing must take part in sports. The academy has seventeen men's and ten women's intercollegiate teams. The football Air Force Falcons count their first really successful season as 1982, when they beat both Army and Navy for the first time.

Although only a small number of cadets become pilots, all are involved in some kind of aviation during their four years at the academy. Seniors who pass the T-41 Pilot Indoctrination Program qualify for pilot training after graduation. Pilots must spend a total of eight years on active duty in the Air Force after they earn their wings. Other academy graduates must stay in the service for five years (six years beginning in 1996). Graduates enter the Air Force as second lieutenants, the lowest officer rank.

Air Force pilots earn their wings after nearly a year of basic and advanced training, a little less for helicopter pilots. Then they join a flying unit, usually for three or four years. After that, they may transfer to a new base and learn to fly a new type of aircraft.

U.S. AIR FORCE RANKS AND INSIGNIA

Commissioned Officers *(lowest to highest)*

Grade

| Second lieutenant | First lieutenant | Captain | Major | Lieutenant colonel |

Colonel   Brigadier general   Major general

Lieutenant general   General   General of the Air Force

Enlisted Personnel *(lowest to highest)*

Grade

Airman   Airman first class   Senior airman   Sergeant   Staff sergeant

Technical sergeant   Master Sergeant   Senior master sergeant   Chief master sergeant

Women are Air Force pilots, too. They are not yet allowed by law to fly in combat, but they pilot all types of jets and support airplanes.

Not every Air Force officer enters the service through the academy. Most come from the Air Force Reserve Officer Training Corps (AFROTC). Students can enroll at 151 college campuses in all fifty states and Puerto Rico. In exchange for a monthly allowance, they must attend certain military classes in addition to their regular studies. When they graduate, they enter the Air Force as second lieutenants. They must spend a minimum of four years on active duty. The Air Force also has a Junior ROTC program for boys and girls who are at least fourteen years old. These young cadets learn about military customs and study aerospace subjects in a three-year program. If they go on to college, they can get credit for a full year in the AFROTC. They are not required to join the Air Force after high school, but if they do, they can enter at a higher pay grade than other enlisted personnel.

★ Enlisted Personnel

All Air Force enlisted personnel are called airmen, whether they are male or female. To enlist, you must be at least eighteen years old, or seventeen with your parents' approval.

The Air Force prefers a high school diploma, but if you don't have one, you may be able to pass tests to qualify.

Once accepted in the Air Force, recruits spend the first six weeks in basic military training (BMT) at Lackland AFB, San Antonio, Texas. There they learn how to adjust to military life. After BMT, most airmen go on to job training at a technical training center. They may spend the next few months learning to be a jet engine mechanic, aerial photographer, weather specialist, or any of the many jobs that the Air

Force offers. If they don't go to a training center, they report directly to a duty station to learn "on the job."

Airmen must enlist for four or six years. Promotions, which mean a higher rating and higher pay, depend on the amount of time they have spent at their current grade and on passing an examination.

A technician repairs a portable recorder.

THE AIR FORCE
THEN AND NOW

Even though it is the youngest of the U.S. military branches, the Air Force can trace its roots back to the Army in World War I, back to the Wright brothers, back to balloons in the Civil War, and even back to the very beginnings of aviation.

Soon after the Civil War began, in 1861, the North had an air force—sort of. It consisted of two balloons. James Allen and William Helme of Rhode Island offered them to the Union to look out for Southern troops. Both balloons were destroyed on launch, however.

The South as well as the North experimented with other balloons during the Civil War. They didn't help either side very much, but balloons later did become part of the U.S. Army. General Adolphus Greely was the Army's chief signal officer from 1887 to 1906. It was his duty to gather and send information for the Army. Greely decided that flight was a good way to get information, so he bought a military balloon from France in 1892. It became the first balloon of the Signal Corps. It was used by American troops in Cuba during the Spanish-

During the Civil War, the Union Army sent this balloon aloft over the Potomac River to observe Confederate troops.

American War, and Greely became known as the "Father of U.S. Military Aviation."

But balloons are lighter than air. What was needed was a solution to the problem of heavier-than-air flight: How to take a machine that is heavier than air, send it aloft, and keep it there under its own power. Many people in many countries for many years tried to do what birds do so easily.

And progress *was* made. Gottlieb Daimler and Karl Benz, two German engineers working independently, built the first internal combustion engines in 1885. That kind of engine, still used today to run automobiles, would become the main source of power for airplanes during the early twentieth century.

Another German, Otto Lilienthal, studied the flight of birds and built gliders. He proved that a curved surface was better than a flat one for aircraft wings.

In the United States, Samuel P. Langley, who was head of the Smithsonian Institution in Washington, D.C., was also trying to build a flying machine. He worked with Alexander Graham Bell, who invented the telephone, and Glenn Curtiss, whose company would later build airplane engines. But Langley's machines were never able to fly, so the mystery of the birds remained a mystery—until 1903 and the Wright brothers.

One might suppose that after so many people had tried for so long to fly, the world would be impressed when the Wrights successfully tested their airplane. Not so. Only three newspapers in the entire United States printed the story! And lots of people didn't believe it even after they'd read it.

Nevertheless, the age of aviation had begun. In 1907, just a few years after the Wrights' first flight, the U.S. Army created the Aeronautical Division within the Signal Corps to deal with "ballooning" and "air machines." The Army asked for bids to build a military plane. It had to carry two people, travel at least 40 miles (64 kilometers) an hour, and stay in the air for no less than sixty minutes.

Not surprisingly, the winners of the competition were Orville and Wilbur Wright. They sold their improved *Flyer* to the Army for $25,000 and received a $5,000 bonus as well. The plane was a success after a tragic beginning that produced the nation's first military air accident. Lieutenant Thomas E. Selfridge, himself an airplane designer, was killed when the plane, piloted by Orville, crashed during its first test flight. Orville suffered broken bones and was in the hospital for two months.

Just before World War I broke out in Europe in 1914, the Army's Aeronautical Division was renamed the Aviation Section. By the end of 1915, the Army boasted fifty-six planes.

The United States did not enter World War I until the spring of 1917. U.S. pilots joined the fight in Europe in August of that year. America's first "ace"—a pilot who has shot down five or more enemy aircraft—was First Lieutenant Edward "Eddie" V. Rickenbacker. The following May the Aviation Section was renamed the Air Service, U.S. Army. It still wasn't an independent branch, but it was no longer part of the Signal Corps.

The war ended on November 11, 1918. The United States and its allies were victorious over Germany and the other Central powers. This, people thought, had been the "war to end all wars." The U.S. military reduced its numbers. The government canceled orders for warplanes. America felt safe with a huge ocean on each side.

But one man, especially, did not think America was safe. His beliefs and persistence dominated aviation in the United States for the next several years. He was Brigadier General William "Billy" Mitchell, an Army pilot who had been born to American parents in France.

After serving in Europe during the war, Mitchell became convinced that air power was the fighting force of the future. As assistant chief of the Air Service, he argued loudly to anyone in government who would listen. Airplanes, said Mitchell, should be used for much more than spying on enemy troops or knocking each other out of the sky. A strong military air force could be the aggressor. An aircraft, declared Mitchell, can sink any surface ship. That last statement especially upset Navy leaders, who believed their biggest ships to be safe from air attack.

Billy Mitchell kept talking. Finally, in 1921, the government gave him permission to prove what he preached. His bombers attacked four captured and unmanned German warships off the Virginia coast. In front of the astonished and embarrassed eyes of government, Navy, and Army leaders, the bombers sank the four German ships in just minutes. Billy Mitchell was right.

But it didn't matter. The military didn't listen. They still didn't listen two years later, when it took Army pilots just two minutes to sink two old U.S. battleships. Billy Mitchell, to say the least, was not very popular with most U.S. military leaders. He was demoted from his post in the Air Service and sent off to a small base in Texas. But he still wouldn't keep quiet. Now he began to speak to the American public. He called the military ''incompetent'' and practically said they should be charged with treason.

In 1925, much to nobody's surprise, Billy Mitchell was called to Washington, D.C., for a court martial, a military trial. He was found guilty of not obeying the orders of his superiors and was suspended

American "ace" Eddie Rickenbacker
led a group of pilots called the Hat in
the Ring Squadron in World War I.

Billy Mitchell (right) with Major General Mason M. Patrick, the first chief of the Army Air Corps.

from military duty for five years. Instead, Mitchell resigned from the Army and traveled around the country urging that the United States change its views on air power.

Billy Mitchell gave up his military career for his belief in air power. And, in the end, the country did listen. Congress passed the Air Corps Act on July 2, 1926. It set up the Army Air Corps, with an allowed force of 1,800 warplanes. The Navy was allowed to keep its own planes to protect its ships, which it still does.

From the 1920s until World War II, the changes in aviation were astounding. New and faster planes were built. Records were broken. In 1923, two pilots made the first nonstop flight across the United States in twenty-six hours and fifty minutes. The next year, Air Service pilots made the first around-the-world flight. Lieutenant Commander Richard E. Byrd and his crew flew to the North Pole in 1926. The old two-wing biplane was replaced by the single-wing monoplane design. The Post Office Department began hiring companies to deliver the mail by air. When the companies began taking passengers along, the airline industry was born. American scientist Robert Goddard tested the first liquid-fueled rocket.

But the most exciting name in aviation during this period belonged to "Lucky Lindy," Charles A. Lindbergh. On May 20–21, 1927, he flew solo nonstop from New York to Paris in his monoplane called *The Spirit of St. Louis*. It took him thirty-three hours, and his daring captured the public imagination. Known as the "Lone Eagle," Lindbergh later flew combat missions in World War II even though he was a civilian.

World War II followed Germany's march across Europe in 1939. The German Air Force, the Luftwaffe, tried to bomb Britain into defeat. Day after day, night after night, German planes pounded British cities and ports in the Battle of Britain. But the Royal Air Force (RAF) proved to have better planes and better pilots. They were successful in turning back the Luftwaffe. Said British Prime Minister Winston Churchill, "Never have so many owed so much to so few."

World War II did not begin for the United States until Japan bombed Pearl Harbor, Hawaii, on December 7, 1941. Eighteen U.S. ships, including all eight battleships, were sunk or damaged that day, and 164 Navy and Army planes were destroyed. The surprise attack was so complete that most of the American planes were destroyed on the ground. President Franklin D. Roosevelt called December 7, 1941, "a date that will live in infamy."

This was the first war in which air power was a major deciding factor. A few months before Pearl Harbor, the U.S. Army's air division was renamed the Army Air Forces. It was headed by General Henry H. "Hap" Arnold, a World War I veteran flyer. By the war's end, the United States would have the world's most powerful air force.

One of the major U.S. air weapons in World War II was the long-range bomber. The B-17 Flying Fortress flew countless bombing raids over Germany. By 1944 the Superfortress, the B-29, had entered the fight against Japan.

Germany surrendered on May 7, 1945, but the Japanese government vowed to fight on until the last soldier. The United States felt that thousands of Americans would lose their lives invading Japan. So President Harry Truman approved the use of America's secret weapon, the atomic bomb. It was dropped from a B-29, the *Enola Gay,* on August 6, 1945, on Hiroshima. In seconds, about 320,000 people were killed. A few days later a second bomb fell on the city of Nagasaki. On August 14, Japan surrendered, and the war was over. The atomic age had begun.

So had the Cold War. This was the period of sword rattling but no actual fighting between the United States and the Soviet Union. Soon after the Air Force became an independent military service in 1947, it played an important role in a tense conflict between the two nations. At war's end, Germany was divided into the Communist-controlled east and the west, dominated by Britain, France, and the United States. The former German capital of Berlin was in the heart of East Germany and was also divided into east and west. In June 1948 the Soviets declared that no supplies could go in and out of the western sector of the city. They wanted to force West Berlin to do as the Communists dictated.

B-17s made countless raids during World War II.

The United States and its allies answered with the Berlin Airlift. Air Force planes, as well as those from the other services and from Great Britain, made more than 275,000 flights into West Berlin. They delivered food and supplies until the Soviet Union called off the blockade on May 12, 1949.

German children wave as a U.S. Air Force plane arrives with supplies during the Berlin Airlift.

The world's next big conflict was the Korean War (1950–1953), fought between Soviet-backed North Korea and U.S.-backed South Korea. A new age had begun for the Air Force, the age of jets. The first jet-versus-jet battle was won by an American Air Force lieutenant, Russell Brown, who shot down a Russian-built MiG-15 in November

1950. In addition to B-29 bombers, the USAF soon had Thunderjets and Saberjets to control the skies. Once again the U.S. Air Force concentrated its efforts against military and industrial targets.

The Korean War ended with a cease-fire in July 1953. Air power had been a key factor in ending the fighting. The Air Force had downed more than one thousand enemy aircraft.

On October 4, 1957, the eyes of the world were focused on a different kind of flying. The United States was severely jolted by the news that the Soviet Union had launched a satellite, *Sputnik I,* into orbit. The world was now in the space age. The Americans responded by launching *Explorer I* on January 31, 1958.

During the next decades, satellites and missiles became an increasingly important part of the Air Force arsenal. Even before *Sputnik,* the Air Force had been working on ICBMs and other missiles. Jet bombers replaced the old reliable B-29s. The powerful B-52 Stratofortress was developed in 1954 and was still flying in the early 1990s.

The Stratofortress was used for fighting in Vietnam. This war was fought in the jungles and mountains of Southeast Asia in the 1960s and early 1970s. The Air Force conducted many bombing raids on North Vietnam. But perhaps its most important flying machine in this conflict was the helicopter. Choppers were especially important in the region's jungle terrain. Armed choppers dropped troops without having to land. They were also used to attack guerrilla forces hidden in the thick jungle.

When the United States withdrew from Vietnam, the Air Force turned much of its focus on the fast-developing technology of the 1980s. New weapons were added to the Air Force mission of keeping the skies safe: the Minuteman and Peacekeeper missiles, and the futuristic-looking B-2 bomber. Work began in the late 1980s on the Advanced Launch System (ALS) program. These new rockets will be flown en-

In 1954, Air Force pilot Charles E. Yeager flew the X-1A faster than the speed of sound. Here he is congratulated by Lawrence Bell, president of the company that built the plane.

Air Force jets on a bombing run over North Vietnam.

Technology played an important role in the 1991 Persian Gulf War. Above, a munitions specialist readies an electronically guided "smart" bomb. At right, the view seen by the electronic guidance system of an F-117 during an attack on an Iraqi target.

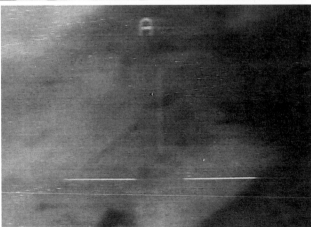

tirely by computers. They are part of the Air Force space program. If they become operational, they may be used to help launch a space station—to be called *Freedom*—that the National Aeronautics and Space Administration hopes to send into orbit in the year 2000.

Air Force technology also played a large role in the 1991 war in the Persian Gulf. The United States and other allies sent forces against Iraq, which had invaded the oil-rich kingdom of Kuwait in the Middle East. Much of this short war was fought in the air. Air Force planes stationed in Saudi Arabia and Navy planes off nearby aircraft carriers flew deep into Iraqi territory. Air Force planes alone flew no fewer than 100,000 sorties against Iraq.

The war in the Persian Gulf is another example of "global reach—global power." In a fast-changing world of new aviation technology, one eye is always on the future. Perhaps with such outbreaks as the Persian Gulf War in mind, Air Force leaders speak of such changes as the first C-17 squadron, Charleston AFB, South Carolina. The C-17 is a "next-generation transport" that can deliver or air drop troops and a vast amount of equipment "anywhere on earth." This huge cargo plane can carry the Army's main battle tank, which weighs sixty-five tons. And, Air Force leaders say, it can do it quicker and on shorter runways than any transport before it.

General Merrill A. McPeak became Air Force chief of staff in 1990. When he was asked to comment on the streamlining of his military department, he said: "We're not starting from scratch. We're building on the shoulders of the many talented and capable people who came before us. We're already the world's best air force."

★ ★ ★

IMPORTANT EVENTS IN
AIR FORCE HISTORY

1907   The U.S. Army sets up the Aeronautical Division as part of the Signal Corps.

1914   The Aviation Section of the Signal Corps takes over aviation training and operation.

1917   The First Aero Squadron arrives in France during World War I; the Aviation Section becomes the Air Service.

1924   Pilots of the Air Service make the first around-the-world flight.

1926   The U.S. Army Air Corps is established.

1941   The Army Air Forces is established, with General Henry H. "Hap" Arnold as the first commander.

1941–
1945   During World War II, the Army Air Forces reaches a peak strength of 80,000 planes.

1945	B-29s drop atomic bombs on the Japanese cities of Hiroshima and Nagasaki to end World War II.
1947	The United States Air Force is established as a separate military service; Captain Charles Yeager breaks the sound barrier in the X-1 rocket-powered aircraft.
1948–1949	Air Force planes deliver supplies to West Berlin during the Berlin Airlift.
1950	The Air Force begins combat operations in the Korean War.
1957	The Air Force launches the first successful intercontinental ballistic missile.
1959	The first class graduates from the Air Force Academy.
1961–1973	U.S. Air Force units take part in the fight against Communist North Vietnam.
1976	The first women are admitted to the Air Force Academy.
1982	The Space Command starts operations in Colorado Springs.
1991	Air Force planes form a major part of the strike force in the Persian Gulf War.

AIR FORCE TALK

Aeronautics—The art or science of flight

Aerospace industry—Manufacture of airplanes, missiles, and other spacecraft

AFB—Air Force Base

Air Force One—747 jet that transports the president of the United States

AIM—Air interceptor missile, used by aircraft against enemy planes

Air-to-surface missile—Missile launched from aircraft at ground target

AWACS—*A*irborne *w*arning *a*nd *c*ontrol *s*ystem: provides all-weather surveillance, command, control, and communications

Ballistic missile—Vehicle that can guide and send itself in a planned direction at a planned speed

Ballistics—Science of missiles

Drone—Aircraft without a pilot; if used for destruction, it is called a missile

Guidance system—The machinery that guides the path of a vehicle

ICBM—*I*nter*c*ontinental *b*allistic *m*issile, largest of the surface-to-surface missiles; can travel from continent to continent

Jet propulsion—Producing motion in one direction by releasing high-pressure gas in another direction

Launch—Sending a rocket-propelled vehicle aloft

MIRV—*M*ultiple *i*ndependently targetable *r*eentry *v*ehicle: an ICBM with nuclear warheads

Mothball—Taking an item, such as an airplane, out of service

National Guard—State units of the Army and Air Force made up of trained civilians; can be ordered into service in national or state emergencies

Rocket—Engine that can produce more power for its size than any other; also, the vehicle that is driven by a rocket engine

Sonic boom—Noise similar to thunder caused by an aircraft, missile, or space shuttle moving faster than sound, or more than 750 miles (1,200 kilometers) per hour at sea level

Stratofortress—Long-range, heavy jet bomber that can fly at high altitudes and has a maximum speed of 650 miles (1,045 kilometers) per hour

Surface-to-surface missile—Missile launched from ground at ground targets

BOOKS FOR FURTHER READING

Malcolm V. Lowe, *Bombers*. Minneapolis: Lerner, 1987.

C. J. Norman, *Military Helicopters*. New York: Watts, 1986.

John Rhea, *The Department of the Air Force*. New York: Chelsea House, 1990.

George Sullivan, *Famous Air Force Bombers*. New York: Dodd, 1985.

K. C. Tessendorf, *Barnstormers and Daredevils*. New York: Macmillan, 1988.

Marcella Thum and Gladys Thum, *Airlift! The Story of the Military Airlift Command*. New York: Dodd, 1986.

INDEX

Page numbers in *italics*
refer to illustrations.

A-10 Thunderbolt II, 27
Advanced Launch System (ALS) program, 52
Aeronautical Division, 42, 43
Air Corps Act of 1926, 46
Aircraft, 16, 22-23, *24, 25,* 25-27, *27,* 28, 51,
   52, *54*
Air Force (*see* U.S. Air Force)
Air Force Falcons, 36
Air Force One, 18
Air Force Reserve Officer Training Corps (AF-
   ROTC), 38
Air interceptor missile (AIM), 31
Airplanes, invention of, 7-8, 42
Air-to-surface missile, 31
Air traffic controllers, *33*
Air University, 20
Allen, James, 40
Arnold, Henry H. "Hap," 48
Atlas launch vehicle, 31
Atomic bomb, 48
Attack and observation planes, 23, 27
Aviation Section, 43

AWACS (E-3 Sentry), 27, *27*

B-1 bomber, 23, *24*
B-2 Stealth bomber, 23, 25
B-17 Flying Fortress, 48, *49*
B-29 Superfortress, 48, 52
B-52 bomber, 22, 23, *24,* 52
Balloons, 22, 40, *41,* 42
Basic training, 38
Bell, Alexander Graham, 42
Bell, Lawrence, *53*
Benz, Karl, 42
Berlin Airlift, 50, *50-51*
Britain, Battle of, 47
Brown, Russell, 51
Byrd, Richard E., 47

C-5A/B Galaxy transport, 28
C-9A Nightingale transport, 28
C-17 transport, 55
Cadet Wing, 35, 36
Chief of naval operations, 14
Churchill, Winston, 47
Civilian Personnel Management Center, 21
Civil War, 22, 40, *41*

Cold War, 48
Commands, 16, 19-21
Congress of the United States, 15
Curtiss, Glenn, 42

Daimler, Gottlieb, 42
Defense, Department of, 12, 14
Direct Reporting Units, 15, 21
Disaster relief, 15

89th Military Airlift Wing, 18
Eisenhower, Dwight D., 35
Enlisted personnel, 38-39, *39*
Enola Gay, 48
Explorer I, 52

F-15, *12-13*
F-15 Eagle, 25
F-16 Fighting Falcon, 25
F-16B Falcon, 8, 10, *10*
F-111 fighter, 22-23, 25
F-117 Stealth fighter, 25, *25, 54*
Field Operating Agencies, 15, 21
Flyer, 8, 43
Freedom space station, 55

Goddard, Robert, 47
Greely, Adolphus, 40, 42

Hat in the Ring Squadron, *44*
Helicopters, 23, 28, *29,* 52
Helme, William, 40
Hiroshima, 48

Intercontinental ballistic missiles (ICBMs), 16,
   31, 52
Internal combustion engine, 42

Joersz, Elden, 26
Joint Chiefs of Staff (JCS), 14

KC-135 Stratotanker, *12-13,* 28
Kitty Hawk, North Carolina, 7, 8
Korean War, 51-52

Langley, Samuel P., 42
Language, 59-60
Lilienthal, Otto, 42
Lindbergh, Charles A. "Lucky Lindy," 47
Luftwaffe, 47

Maverick missile, 31
McPeak, Merrill A., 55
MiG-15 fighter, 51
Minorities, 35
Minuteman missile, *17,* 52
Missiles, 16, *17,* 22, 28, *30,* 31, 52
Mitchell, William "Billy," 43, 45-46, *46*

Nagasaki, 48
National Aeronautics and Space Administration
   (NASA), 11, 19, 55
National Military Establishment, 12
National Security Act of 1947, 11

Officers, 32, 35-36, 38

Pacific Air Force, 21
Patrick, Mason M., *46*
Peacekeeper missile, *30,* 31, 52
Pearl Harbor, 47-48
Pentagon, 15
Persian Gulf War, 15, 16, *54,* 55
President's plane, 18

Radar, 23, 25
Reconnaissance planes, 23, 26, 27
Rickenbacker, Edward "Eddie" V., 43, *44*
Roosevelt, Franklin D., 48
Royal Air Force (RAF), 47

Saberjets, 52
Satellites, 52
Secretary of defense, 14
Secretary of the Air Force, 14
Selfridge, Thomas E., *9,* 43
Sidewinder missile, 31
Signal Corps, 40, 42, 43
"Smart" bombs, 25, *54*

Spaatz, Carl "Tooey," 14
Space program, 11, 19, 31, 52, 55
Space Transportation System (STS), 31
Spanish-American War, 40, 42
Special-duty aircraft, 23, 27
Spirit of St. Louis, The, 47
Sputnik I, 52
Squadrons, 22-23
SR-71 (Blackbird), 26, *26*
Strategic Air Command, 16
Surface-to-surface missile, 31
Symington, Stuart, 14

T-37 Tweet, 28
Tactical Air Command, 16
Tankers, 23, 28
Thunderbirds, 10
Thunderjets, 52
Titan launch vehicle, 31
Trainers, 23, 28
Transports, 23, 28
Truman, Harry, 11, 48

UH-IN Iroquois helicopter, 28
Union Army, 40, *41*
U.S. Air Force
    aircraft, 16, 22-23, *24, 25,* 25-27, *27,* 28,
        51, 52, *54*
    commands, 16, 19-21
    Congress and, 15
    creation of, 11, 12
    enlisted personnel, 38-39, *39*
    headquarters of, 15
    in Korean War, 51-52
    language, 59-60
    minorities in, 35
    missiles, 16, *17,* 22, 28, *30,* 31, 52
    mission of, 11, 52
    Mitchell and, 43, 45-46, *46*
    officers, 32, 35-36, 38
    in Persian Gulf War, 15, 16, *54,* 55
    reorganization of, 16
    seal of, *14*
    space program and, 11, 19, 31, 52, 55

in Vietnam War, 52, *53*
women in, 35, 38
in World War I, 43
in World War II, 47-48, *49*
U.S. Air Force Academy at Colorado Springs,
    21, 32, *34,* 35-36
U.S. Air Force chief of staff, 14
U.S. Air Force Combat Command, 16, *17*
U.S. Air Force District of Washington, 21
U.S. Air Force Intelligence Command, 19
U.S. Air Force Matériel Command, 19
U.S. Air Force National Guard, 15
U.S. Air Force Operational Test and Evalua-
    tion Center, 21
U.S. Air Force Reserve, 15, 21
U.S. Air Forces in Europe, 21
U.S. Air Force Space Command, 19
U.S. Air Force Special Operations Command,
    19
U.S. Air Force Training Command, 19-20, *20*
U.S. Air Force Weather Service, 21
U.S. Air Mobility Command, 19
U.S. Army, 8, 11, 12, 14, 40, 42, 43
U.S. Army Air Corps, 46
U.S. Coast Guard Academy at New London,
    35
U.S. Marine Corps, 11, 12, 14
U.S. Military Academy at West Point, 35
U.S. Naval Academy at Annapolis, 35
U.S. Navy, 11, 12, 46

Vietnam War, 52, *53*

War Department, 12
Wings, 21
Women, 35, 38
World War I, 43
World War II, 47-48, *49*
Wright, Orville, 7-8, *9,* 10, 42, 43
Wright, Wilbur, 7-8, 10, 42, 43

X-1A, *53*

Yeager, Charles E., *53*